Legal Limericks

By Donald S. Altschul, Esq.

SURVIVAL SERIES PUBLISHING COMPANY

Legal Limericks are published by:

      The Survival Series Publishing Company, P.O. Box 77313, San Francisco, California 94107 If your local bookstore is out, you may order additional copies through the publisher by sending $9.95 + $1.00 S/H per book to the above address.

This book is not intended as legal advice. The limericks in this book do not necessarily represent the current state of the law, and are only an expression of the opinion of the court in the cases relied upon.

Editorial Consultant:	Rudy Hirota
Desktop Publishing:	Katherine Asada
Book & Cover Design:	Jeffrey Adachi
Illustrations:	Dover Publications, Inc.

FOREWARD BY U.S. SENIOR JUDGE JOHN L. KANE

In my years on the bench, I have endeavored to inject a little humor into the grim and drudging prose of judicial opinions, especially in those cases which present opportunities which are too tempting to abjure. Don Altschul's *Legal Limericks* take legal humor to another level altogether, but yet preserve the purity of the art form, by creating a series of five-line short stories with alternate rhyming verses, ending with an anapest, a three-syllable foot with the accent on the third syllable --- dih-dih-DAH dih-dih-DAH. But a limerick isn't a sonnet; its supposed to be fun, not hidebound to some steely consistency. So read Altschul and laugh!

John L. Kane, Jr.
U.S. Senior District Judge

Table of Contents

The promoters of a men-against-hen race were not liable for injuries to participants, who had freely chosen to compete for prizes.

He raced after chickens one day,

and broke a leg. Should sponsor pay?

No. His lively gumption

made risk his assumption.

He chose to engage in fowl play.

McLeod Store v. Vinson
213 Ky. 667, 281 S.W. 799 (1926)

Although the owner of a donkey may have been negligent in tying its feet and turning it on to a public road, that owner could successfully sue the driver whose wagon, moving at a high speed, ran into the animal and killed it.

A slow-moving wagon might pass

an animal fettered in grass.

Since you chose high speed,

you pay for his dead steed.

In future, Mann, just watch your ass.

Davies v. Mann
10 Mees. & W. 545; 152 Eng. Rep. 588 (Ex. 1842)

The family of a man who was in a fatal night-time car crash could not recover damages, because the man broke the law and endangered himself by driving without lights.

Decedent, while driving at night,

broke the law by not driving with light.

Said Justice Cardozo:

"[Now, listen up, bozo,

what you did was worse than not bright!]"

Martin v. Herzog
228 N.Y. 164 (1920)

A pregnant cow believed by its owner to be barren was sold for $80. The owner had a right to cancel the sale if he and the buyer had agreed to the sale only because they both thought the cow incapable of breeding.

For this beef-cow who carried a calf,

the 80-buck price was a gaffe.

The injustice moves us,

and so, it behooves us

to say: Here's a cow-and-a-half.

Sherwood v. Walker,
66 Mich 568, 33 N.W. 919 (1887)

A minor may successfully deny the validity of his contracts.

The court said: For sure, it's a pity

that this lad than you was more witty.

It must be our finding:

The kid's word ain't binding.

You take the loss, plaintiff. Tough t-tty.

Keser v. Chagnon
159 Colo. 209 (1966)

Noting that the law criminalizing sexual intercourse with under-age females was intended to cut down on teenage pregnancy, defendant introduced evidence of his vasectomy to show he was incapable of causing the harm the law was enacted to prevent. The court upheld the judgment convicting him of the crime.

Of all rape defenses we've stocked up,

here's the best: I could not get her knocked up.

Though defendant was spermless,

we can't let him squirm less:

He did the act, that gets him locked up.

People v. Langdon
192 Cal.App.3d 148 (1987)

Because a guilty plea in a criminal proceeding did not afford a "full presentation" of the case, it was held inadmissible in a later civil suit on the same facts. For the same reason, the husband was not "estopped" [prevented] from forcing his wife to present evidence on the issue in the civil suit.

For full proof, civil plaintiff can't seize

on her hubby's prior crim'nal court pleas.

What he told some cop'll

not bring forth estoppel.

We must reverse. Mind our cues, Pease.

Pease v. Pease
201 Cal.App.3d 29 (1988)

Mrs. Risk, a Norwegian citizen, got financial aid and other help from her government to violate a California court order by taking her children to Norway and concealing them from their father. The father lost his suit against the Norwegian government and its officials, because their acts were within normal consular discretion and acceptable under Norwegian law.

Her kidnapping maneuver was brisk.

Her homeland supported her fisc.

And even though Norway held open its doorway,

a nation's immune from this, Risk.

Risk v. Halvorseen
936 F.2d 393 (9th Cir. 1991)

In this landmark case, the United States Supreme Court ruled that the fruits of an illegal arrest or search by police cannot be used against a criminal defendant unless the taint of illegality is sufficiently removed by intervening circumstances.

We weed out, with reasoned restraint,

what's admissible here from what ain't

Here, one technicality

yields illegality

where fruits aren't purged of the taint.

Wong Sun v. United States,
 371 U.S. 471 (1963)

The court, with a nod to the Daniel Webster legend, found itself compelled to dismiss this lawsuit because there was no proof that defendant was subject to its territorial power.

Instructionless, we can't stride straight in

and serve pauper's pleadings on Satan.

When we've jurisdiction

o'er fiends from old fiction,

then Hades will feature ice-skatin'.

United States ex rel. Mayo v. Satan and his Staff
54 F.R.D. 282 (W.D. Pa 1971)

Mrs. Palsgraf, standing on a railroad platform near a penny scale, was hit by the scale when it was jarred loose after explosives fell from the grasp of a passenger being pulled onto a train by a porter. The court said that the "orbit of danger" for which the railroad was accountable did not extend as far as the scale, and so found the railroad was not liable for Palsgraf's injury.

Cardozo held: Plaintiff here fails

to prove duty which our rule entails.

To "orbit of danger"

she was remote stranger.

Palsgraf must bear weight of the scales.

Palsgraf v. Long Island Railroad
248 N.Y. 339, 162 N.E. 99 (1928)

The widow and son of the actor who portrayed Dracula in movies could not stop the producers from selling the actor's likeness after his death, because the right of privacy protects only a living individual, and is not an asset handed down to heirs.

Heirs of Dracula-star saw deep red

when the studio's tills stayed well-fed

selling Bela's grim face.

Their complaint's out-of-place.

Privacy just protects the undead.

Lugosi v. Universal Pictures
25 Cal.3d 813 (1979)

Titan, the maker of a water-safety valve, was held subject to being sued in Illinois for an injury that happened there, even though the valve was not sold in Illinois but sold to a heater-manufacturer who did business there.

Juridical strictures we lighten,

a tort-victim's fortunes to brighten.

Our conscience we salve

as we close down the valve

on such negligence as that of Titan.

Gray v. American Radiator & Standard Sanitary Corp.
22 Ill. 432 (1961)

Hayes helped his friend (Hill) break into a store from which Hill handed out a side of bacon. Hayes was not guilty of burglary, because Hill was a relative of the store-owner and had no intent to actually steal.

The trial court here was quite mistaken

in this conspiratorial break-in.

Where the store-owner's friend

had no criminal end,

prosecution can't bring home the bacon.

State v. Hayes,
105 Ms. 76, 16 S.W. 514 (1891)

When the National Enquirer published a story falsely asserting Clint Eastwood's romantic involvement with a country singer, Eastwood could successfully sue for invasion of his common-law right of privacy.

A newspaper chose falsely to say

with whom big movie star chose to play.

When they did not get right

who he slept with at night,

court let actor demand: Make my day.

Eastwood v. Superior Court
149 Cal.App.3d 409 (1983)

In upholding a law requiring a life sentence for a three-time felon as applied to a man whose three non-violent crimes involved property worth less than $240 total, the court said that states had an absolute right to make such laws, but admitted that life imprisonment for multiple parking tickets would probably offend the constitutional ban on cruel and unusual punishment.

He passed a check backed with elastic,

and forged a name on stolen plastic,

then took cash for work

he decided to shirk.

We hold a life term's not too drastic.

Rummel v. Estelle
445 U.S. 263 (1980)

After suffering throat injury from a one-inch chicken bone that was in his chicken enchilada, a customer sued the restaurant. The California Supreme Court overruled the lower courts and found the restaurant negligent for the overlooked chicken bone.

Because lunch shouldn't injure the throat,
we rule, by a five-to-two vote:
Those who sell fowl food
still deserve to be sued,
and the lower courts here just missed the boat.

The trial court made a few small errata
when it ruled: "Injured diner gets *nada*."
To adjust we make haste,
and so find, in good taste,
courts can't throw out the whole enchilada.

Mexicali Rose v. Superior Court
1 Cal.4th 617 (1992)

Beware of uninsured bathtubs!

A woman knocked over during a collegiate bathtub race could not collect from the insurance policy which covered the driver while in an "automobile."

Ms. Horne was unable to hasten

from the paths of some youths bathtub-racin'.

Though for plaintiff we feel.

the word "automobile"

can't be held to insure four-wheeled basin.

Horne v. Geico
132 Ga.App. 230; 297 S.E.2d 663 (reh. den. 1974)

A city-owned golf course was liable for injury to a golfer on a defective cart, despite a contractual disclaimer of responsibility, because the city and the golfer were not on equal footing in creating the terms of the contract.

The rental-cart's brakes took no speed off.

Your disclaimer can't write his need off.

Your bargaining power

o'er his here did tower.

Pay up to this golfer so teed off!

Baker v. City of Seattle
79 Wash.2d 198, 484 P.2d 405

A contract for sale of a "chicken" did not bar the seller from providing "stew" chicken instead of the young broilers or fryers the buyer expected. The court's opinion, which opened with the first line of this limerick, held that the buyer had failed to meet its burden of proof, as the party bringing the lawsuit, that the contract used "chicken" to mean something narrower than its standard definition.

"The issue is, what is [a] chicken?"
Our judicial nose we must now stick in.
Defendant inquires:
"Are hens always fryers?"
That doubt here has made our plot thicken.

The plaintiff's implicit relying
that only young birds they'd be buying
left them deeply ruing
they got birds for stewing,
too old for good broiling or frying.

The burden of proof leaves its load
on the plaintiff. Here, federal code
clearly gives us the word
that a bird is a bird.
Plaintiff's "chicken" does not cross that road.

Frigaliment Importing Co. v. B.N.S. Int'l Sales Corp.
190 F. Supp. 116 (S.D.N.Y. 1960)

A robber whose victim died of a heart attack was properly convicted of first-degree murder.

Though to rob at gunpoint may seem smart,

it might cause heavy punishment's start.

We'll charge "Murder One"

if, when scared by the gun,

the victim stops working his heart.

People v. Stamp
2 Cal.App.2d 203 (1969)

The patron of an amusement park ride that obviously causes people to fall down couldn't sue for his fractured kneecap. The last line is taken directly from Chief Justice Cardozo's ruling.

He got on a ride called the "Flopper,"
which was advertised as a whopper
The ride's sudden jerk
caused his knee not to work.
He sued, saying safeguards were improper.

Adventuresome men like to roam
exploring cave and catacomb.
If you go for a ride,
you must pay when you slide,
"The timorous may stay at home."

Murphy v. Steeplechase Amusement Co.
250 N.Y. 479, 166 N.E. 173 (1929)

Game show hostess Vanna White was allowed to sue under the Lanham Act [15 U.S.C. § 1125(a)] on the "likelihood of confusion" that a home entertainment ad featuring a robot dressed in her style could imply her endorsement of the product.

A game-show star started a tiff,

when a jeweled and wigged mannequin, stiff,

with a look like the star's,

tried to sell VCR's.

Held: A jury might not know the diff.

White v. Samsung Electronics America
971 F.2d 1395 (9th Cir., 1992)

When software professional Eugene Wang left his job at Borland and went to a rival company, his former employers sued, claiming theft of trade secrets.

When his phone with new job-promise rang,

With big secrets the E-mail lines sang,

sharing data all true.

This just made Borland stew,

and they put a hard grip on their Wang.

Symantec v. Eubanks
pending case

A woman who felt a live worm crawling on her lip as she drank from a bottle of Coke was entitled to sue for breach of warranty.

Ms. Nock felt intestinal strife

From her soft drink, invertebrate-rife.

A soda with worms

defies warranty's terms,

even though buyer knows "Coke adds life."

Nock v. Coca-Cola Bottling
156 A. 537, 102 Pa. Super. 515 (1931)

The court upheld a 3-million-dollar judgement against a railroad company, whose train killed a married trucker when it hit him.

Dear railroad: You must pay big buck.

Your train killed the trucker it struck.

Three Mill's not excessive.

It would be oppressive

to rule widow flat, out of Lueck.

Southern Pacific Transp. Co. v. Lueck
111 Ariz. 560, 535 P.2d 599 (1975)

A man who died in a car crash without leaving a will was for 24 years married to and had children with different wives. The court upheld the equal division of his estate between the widow, on the principle that the "innocent wives" were entitled to equal shares of the property acquired during the bigamous marriages.

He'd lived a lie, led dual existence,

He'd paid for two families' subsistence.

It's now only fair

Widows equally share.

Let each wife more cautiously tryst hence.

Estate of Vargas
36 Cal.App.3d 714 (1974)

A pet owner is liable for injuries to others caused by his pet.

His talking bird, in Carolina,

Caught rabies and bit his friend Dinah.

The court made him pay

for her wounds of that day,

holding liable his lunatic mynah.

Restatement of Torts §507

The rule against perpetuities which has mystified generations of lawyers and law students is "that no interest in property is good unless it must vest, if at all, not later than 21 years plus period of gestation, after some life or lives in being at time of creation of interest." Under Florida law, a lawyer who does not understand this rule has been held not guilty of malpractice.

"Does law school expose ambiguities?"

[he asked.]   I said: "I've seen a few o'dese.

On my temper it grates that the law of estates

boils down to one rule: No perpetuities."

4 Restatement of Real Property §370

A federal statute to enforce an international treaty was held to pre-empt state law on the hunting of birds migrating between the U.S. and Canada. The supremacy of federal law was held to outweigh the Tenth Amendment doctrine of reserving power to the states.

Of precedents we could cite herds

just to show that the treaty-power's words

give ample endorsement

to acts of enforcements.

State's claim is unjust for the birds.

Missouri v. Holland
252 U.S. 416 (1920)

The court invalidated a San Francisco laundry-regulating ordinance which, by its structure, restricted only the operation of laundries run by Asians.

When City Hall unfairly implants

different rules on pressers of pants,

to the Asian races

the law has two faces.

Everyone's got to have the same chance.

Yick Wo v. Hopkins,
116 U.S. 356 (1885)

Defendant unsuccessfully claimed that he lacked the required <u>mens rea</u>, or guilty state of mind, because he believed the woman he had sex with was of legal age. The court defined the crime as having sex with an under-age female, regardless of whether her age was known.

Prince was a red-blooded male,
but he overlooked one minor detail.
Regarding his date
She was too young to mate
A fact that fractured his fairy tale.

Prince Charming said "How can this be?
To me she looked twenty-three."
The court said "That's too bad.
In the future, my lad,
Be sure to check Snow White's I.D."

Regina v. Prince
13 Cox's Crim. Cases (1875)

The family of a murder victim sought payment from the killer's homeowner's insurance. Because the insurance expressly denied coverage for a "loss ... willfully caused by the policyholder," the court said the insurer was not required to pay.

Though for his deed he had to do time,
victim's kin wanted cash for the crime.
When they asked for a fee
from his home policy,
his insurer would not pay a dime.

The case hinges on one little fact
stated in the insurer's pact:
There is no compensation
For harm done with intention
And murder's a deliberate act.

State Farm Fire & Casualty Co. v. Byrd,
729 F.Supp. 1265 (N.D. Cal. 1990)

The city was not liable for the failure of its spillway system to prevent damage from a flood of unprecedented, and therefore unforeseeable, proportions.

The waters flooded the city.

The damage caused was a pity.

If nature's the cause

God's beyond reach of laws

Victim's can't sue a deity.

City of Piqua v. Morris
120 N.E. 300 (1918)

A person whose limb was paralyzed could not get a disability benefit that the policy limited to "loss of member."

Though he'd paid his full premium's cost,

he had not read each "T" that he'd crossed.

A paralyzed limb

won't require payment, Jim,

when they just pay for limbs that are lost.

Suarez v. Live Ins. Co. of N.A.
206 Cal.App.3d 1396 (1988)

In this case, two "drinking buddies" got into a barroom dispute which resulted in Mr. Castro's biting off the ears and nose of Mr. Maestas. After Castro was convicted of that crime, Maestas sued him for negligence, attempting to get money from Castro's homeowner's policy that covered negligent acts. Denying that claim, the court ruled: "[T]hree bites do not a negligence case make." In the last verse, the author suggests that the insurers are not apt to pay for the behavior of people like the cannibal protagonist in Silence of the Lambs.

Though alcohol often endears
friend to friend, there are times, it appears,
when booze-induced feeling
requires further healing
as here, of a nose and two ears.

Two once friendly local-pub crawlers
turned into incensed brutal brawlers.
When tempters did settle,
they showed their true mettle
by being insurance-firm callers.

The court finds it must be a rejecter
of this homeowner's-coverage-expecter.
Biting off nose and ear
isn't negligence, dear.
You're not "in good hands" with Dr. Lecter.

West American Ins. Co. v. Maestas,
631 F. Supp. 1565 [D. Colo., 1986]

Insurance that made mortgage payments any time the insured was "disabled," that is, under a doctor's care, was held not obligated to pay the insured's widow. The limerick's last 11 words are quoted directly from the opinion.

The young couple got mortgage-insured.
Widow thought that her coverage endured.
That gives too much agility
to "disability"
With death, liability's cured.

Though the world occurs inside one's head,
we can't oft get what is from what's said.
The lesson for gleaning?
"A word has no meaning ..."
"... he was not disabled, but dead."

Silva v. Aetna Life Ins. Co.
196 Cal.App.3d 789 (1987)

The court unanimously upheld a law banning "offensive, derisive or annoying speech" as applied to a Jehovah's Witness who, after getting knocked to the ground by his listeners, used the quoted language to a marshall removing him from the scene.

He spoke beliefs which he held dear,

damned the God of those who gathered near,

got beat up for his pains.

Why was he put in chains?

He called a cop a "damned racketeer."

Chaplinsky v. New Hampshire
315 U.S. 568 (1942)

A smoke-ball manufacturer whose advertisement promised to pay 50 pounds to anyone who used their flu treatment unsuccessfully was required to pay Carlill, whose purchase and use of the product was held to be full performance of her part of an offered contract.

Carbolic said, "It's a revolution!
Flu sufferers we have your solution.
Just inhale our smoke
and to prove it's no joke
50 pounds says this cure's no illusion.

Ms. Carlill bought Carbolic's potion
and followed directions with devotion.
But when the smoke cleared
the flu still appeared
which set the litigation in motion.

The court said that Carbolic's ad
presents a contract that's iron-clad.
We see through the smoke screen,
now cough up the green
To all the people who have been had.

Carlill v. Carbolic Smoke Ball Co.
1 Q.B. 256 (1893)

Dr. Protopappas, a dentist, was prosecuted for a series of deaths among his patients due to over-anesthetization. The first, who suffered from lupus, weighed only 88 pounds and received an amount of anesthesia excessive for her weight. A teenager with enlarged tonsils received anesthesia at the hands of the dentist's assistant, who was not licensed to administer it. The final verse advises dentists to either be more circumspect, or to adopt the non-anesthetic practices of the sadistic dentist in "Little Shop of Horrors."

This crazy I.V.-popping bounder
doped up a frail 88-pounder.
At her cardiac arrest
he for sure could have guessed.
He left her more blue than he found her.

When the large-tonsilled teen he did wave in
(whose wisdom teeth were beyond savin'),
the dosage, persistent,
was pumped by assistant
unlicensed for such misbehavin'.

Though he'd tried to keep pained folks mellow,
the court found him no jolly good fellow.
Ease a patient's distress?
Better think twice, I guess,
or go no-drug, like Orin Scrivello.

People v. Protopappas
201 Cal.App.3d 152 (1988)

After a court trial, the judge ordered that $1.4 million in damages be paid to the estate of children's author Dr. Seuss by a T-shirt manufacturer who sold shirts depicting a marijuana-smoking Cat in the Hat without permission.

If a world-famous image you pinch
without consent, the result is a cinch:
When you're caught someday
you'll be required to pay
and your profits will go to the Grinch.

In putting an end to this scam,
not all entrepreneurs do we damn.
But you must pay a fee
for someone else's creativity
there's a price for Green Eggs and Ham.

Geisel v. Unger
(92-1067-CV-W-1, 5/ /93; W.D. Mo.)

The Survival Series
Legal Limericks T-Shirts
only $12.95!

Each T-shirt comes with a humorous eye-catching illustration on the front & a smart Limerick on your back!

Please indicate the quantity, style and size (Large or Extra-Large only)!

_____ *Palsgraf* Limerick T-shirts   L   X-L

_____ *Pregnant Cow* Limerick   L   X-L

Send $12.95 + $2.00 S/H for each T-shirt.
Please allow four weeks for delivery.

Name:_____

Address: _____

City/State: _____ Zip: _____

WORRIED ABOUT LAW SCHOOL?
Defuse Your Fears With
THE FIRST YEAR LAW SCHOOL SURVIVAL KIT

Learn everything you need to make it through law school.

How to: •Read and brief cases • Prepare for the Socratic method of teaching •Outline •Analyze and Solve law school exam problems

Also includes: •Five problem solving approaches in each of the first year subjects, setting forth the black letter law in a simple and concise format •Memory mnemonics, color codes and visual graphics for easy memorization •Over fifty examples of model questions and answers

DON'T GAMBLE WITH YOUR CAREER!

The Bar Exam Survival Kit
By Jeff Adachi

Increase your odds of passing with
THE BAR EXAM SURVIVAL KIT

- mnemonic devices and over 200 illustrations make learning the law fun
- complete black letter law coverage of all multistate subjects
- step by step instruction on writing a winning bar exam answer
- ideal for last minute cramming
- the last step of bar preparation
- 10 day full money-back guarantee!

"The best guide to getting through the bar exam I have ever seen."
-Professor Peter G. Keane, Hastings College of the Law

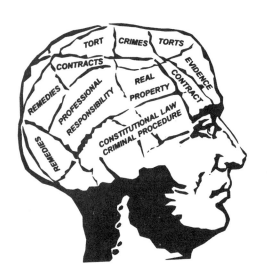

We hope you enjoyed this book. If you are interested in learning about other Survival Series products, please mail in this coupon. Thank you!

Please send me my **FREE** copy of *How to Write Winning Law School Examination Answers* at no cost. Also Please RUSH my order for:

_____ copies of *The First Year Law School Survival Kit*
_____ copies of *The California Bar Exam Survival Kit*
_____ copies of *The Bar Exam Survival Kit*
_____ copies of *The Survival Series Flashcard Book*

$39.95 per book. Please add $4.00 shipping and handling per book, California residents add 8.5% sales tax.

Name: _____

Address: _____

City: _____

State: _____ Zip: _____

Place this card in a properly stamped and addressed envelope and mail to: The Survival Series, P.O. Box 77313, San Francisco, CA 94107

Introducing: The 1994 National Legal Limerick Contest

If this book pleased you a bit,
please try to contribute to it.
Invest your own time
in a legal-case rhyme - -
We'll pay you if we deem it fit.

The Survival Series Publishing Company

If you have a Legal Limerick you'd like to enter, please complete the following form and mail to:

The 1994 National Legal Limerick Contest
The Survival Series Publishing Company
P.O. Box 77313
San Francisco, CA 94107

Please include the full citation of the case upon which the Limerick is based. All entries must be received no later than December 25, 1994. Submissions not used will not be returned. The Survival Series will pay $25.00 for each Legal Limerick used. Good luck and have fun!

My favorite Legal Limerick was:_____

I am a   LAW STUDENT   LAWYER   HUMAN BEING   LAWYER HATER
                                        ⌈Circle One Only⌉

I could definitely be convinced to spend a few hard earned dollars on the next Legal Limerick book.

_____True Beyond a Reasonable Doubt
_____True by a Preponderance of Evidence
_____Only if I Promise Never to Laugh Again
_____Yes, under Penalty of Perjury

I am interested in learning about other Survival Series publications:

_____*The Bar Exam Survival Kit*
_____*The First Year Law School Survival Kit*
_____*The Survival Series Flashcard Book*

Name: _____

Address: _____

About the Author

During his 20 year career as a professional writer, Donald Altschul has seen his work published in *Show Business, California Prisoner, Reform Judaism,* and other regional and national media. Altschul, whose law practice includes California and New York, is a graduate of Stanford University and Rutgers School of Law/Newark. He has appeared before the federal District Court and Court of Appeals, as well as the Supreme Court of the United States.

During his decade of lawyering, he has served on the Board of Directors of the Prisoners' Rights Union has maintained a private practice in San Francisco, where he has lived since 1981. He has worked as an improvisational comedian and as befits any author, has a job history spanning sales of encyclopedias, health insurance, annuities, water treatment systems and cosmetics.